Encore

Note: Those titles marked (*) are **brand new arrangements** and do not appear in any other Fred Bock organ collection.

en-core/än-ˌkō(ə)r/*noun* a demand for repetition or reappearance made by an audience: a further performance in response to such a demand.

Reading this definition makes me think the title for this book was well-chosen! 50 of my best organ arrangements were carefully selected to bring you a wide variety of styles and titles. All of them are performed enough to warrant inclusion in a compilation of this nature. Some may well say that they have other collections which contain a few of the titles in this book. Alas, 'tis true. But what you *don't* have is all the brand new arrangements available *only in this book!* I know you will love the rich harmonies of EL-SHADDAI and IN THIS VERY ROOM, and the tenderness of THOU ART WORTHY. And then there's a very extra special treatment of JESUS LOVES ME. Some of you may already know my piano setting of this song coupled with Debussy's "Clair de Lune;" well, now, here it is, for the first time ever, in an organ setting; and it works quite nicely, too. The pedal part is not demanding at all, and there's even a spot where you home organists can use a percussion stop... which brings me to the next selection, I AM A PROMISE. This popular Gaither song for kids (big and little) is my personal favorite in the book. I spent lots of hours on this one, folks, so be careful to play the notes just as I done writed 'em down! The intro starts the ball rolling and then that strong melody just roars on through. Watch those accidentals so the chords are really right and tight! Sightread this one on your own time! While the value of this for a church service is somewhat debatable, it sure is a fun piece to play, and every time I do, I feel a strong urge to go out for pizza! On the last note of the piece I added a cymbal crash in the pedal, just in case you happen to get to run through this little ditty some day at Radio City Music Hall. I suggest this as a postlude for the *last* Sunday at your church!

I hope you enjoy playing these little creations of mine over and over again. Encore! Encore! Bravo! *Encore!*

FRED BOCK
December 1984

JESUS LOVES ME

(Based on "Clair de Lune")

Hammond Organs

Upper: 00 2706 002 (*)
Lower: F♯ preset or 00 4524 012
Pedal: 52

Other Organs

Upper: Flutes 4', 2', Sw. to Sw. 4'(*)
Lower: Strings 8', 4' and celestes
Pedal: Light Flute 16'

WILLIAM BRADBURY and
CLAUDE DEBUSSY
Arranged by Fred Bock

(*) If a percussion stop is available on upper manual, this should be used where indicated. It could be added and removed from the suggested registration or put on a separate preset piston on the upper manual.

mf
f
slowly rolled
Sw.
ten.
ten.
ten.
percussion on
mp
Gt.
percussion off
rit.
pp
a little faster
sustained
mf
Sw.
mf
mf

mf
accelerando
mp
Gt.
mf
Sw.
Sw.
Gt.
mp
8va
Sw.
slowly rolled
percussion on
p

percussion off
Like the beginning
Sw.
Gt.
pp
mp
L.H.
R.H.
ten.
crescendo & accelerando
mf
f
Slowly
8va
ppp

THOU ART WORTHY

Hammond Organs

Upper: F♯, G♯, or A♯
00 6760 330
B 00 0603 000
Lower: A♯ 00 6746 324

Pedal: 53

Tab Organs

Upper: Oboe 8′, or light reed solo stop
Prepare: Flute 4′, trem
Lower: Strings and Flutes and celestes, 8′, 4′
Pedal: Light Flute 16′, 8′ Bourdon 16′

Words and Music by
PAULINE MICHAEL MILLS
Arranged by Fred Bock

Sw.
pow'r! For Thou hast cre - a - ted, hast all things cre - a - ted, For
Thou hast cre - a - ted all things;
Gt.
And for Thy pleas-ure
f
accented
optional D.C.
they are cre - a - ted, For Thou art wor - thy, Thou art wor - thy,
f
ff
ten.
Sw. Flute 4′, tremolo
p
Thou art wor - thy, O Lord.
l.h.
Gt.
mp

EL-SHADDAI

Hammond Organs		Tab Organs	
Upper:	D♯ or 00 3703 000	Upper:	Flute 4′ Tremolo optional
Lower:	F♯ or 00 5624 222	Lower:	Strings 8′, 4′ Celestes as needed
Pedal:	42	Pedal:	Light 16′ Flute

Words and Music by
JOHN THOMPSON and MICHAEL CARD
Arranged by Fred Bock

age You're still the same by the pow - er of the Name. El - Shad - dai, El - Shad -
dai, Er - kam - ka - na A - do - nai, we will praise and lift You high, El-Shad-
dai.
loco both times

Smoothly building
ff
1.
ad lib.
Gt.
f
2.
Gt.
f
ff
f
ritard.
mf
mp
p
pp

BECAUSE HE LIVES

Hammond Organs
UPPER: A♯ 00 5508 000
LOWER: A♯ 00 3403 110
PEDAL: 42
Vibrato off

other Organs
UPPER: Light String 8′
Strong Flutes 4′, 2′
LOWER: Strings 8′, 4′
PEDAL: Bourdon 16′
Vibrato off

Words by
GLORIA & WILLIAM J. GAITHER

Music by
WILLIAM J. GAITHER
Arr. Fred Bock

*Add 8′ Flute for added strength, if necessary - Hammond: 00 5808 000.

3
know He holds the fu - ture, and life is
1
ten. ten. ten.
worth the liv - ing just be-cause He lives.
ff
ten.
ten. ten.
ten. ten.
2
8va
loco
slowing to end
ff
mf

I AM A PROMISE

Hammond Organs

Upper: B 00 7870 345
Percussion on, Fast, Second
Prepare: A♯ 00 7808 456

Lower: A♯ 00 6736 002
Pedal: 64

Tab Organs

Upper: Flutes 8′, 2′ Harp on, Glockenspiel percussion
Prepare: Full strings and flutes and diapasons 8′, 4′, 2′

Lower: Supportive Strings and Flutes
Pedal: Flutes 16′, 8′, Gt to Ped.

Words and Music by
GLORIA and WILLIAM J. GAITHER
Arranged by Fred Bock

In a bright shuffle tempo (♩=100)

great big bun-dle of po-ten-ti - al - i - ty. And I am
learn-ing to hear God's voice, and I am try-ing to
make the right choices, I'm a prom-ise to be an - y - thing God wants me to be.
Sw. (alternate setting)
I can go an - y - where that He wants me to go, I can

* If playing a 3 manual organ, play countermelody on another manual/setting.

Suddenly faster, 1920's feel (♩=138)

HOW GREAT THOU ART

HAMMOND

Upper: 01 8876 334
Full Vibrato
Lower: 00 7845 223
Full Vibrato
Pedal: 54

SPINET

Upper: 01 8876 334
Full Vibrato
Lower: 7845 2230
Full Vibrato
Pedal: 5

OTHERS

Upper: Full Swell except
5 1/3' & 16' Tremolo
Lower: Strgs, Flutes & Diapason 8'
Pedal: Gt. to Ped. Bourdon 16'

Arranged by
FRED BOCK

STUART K. HINE

Eb
roll - ing thun - der, Thy pow'r through - out the un - i - verse dis -
Bb F7
Bb
played. Then sings my soul my Sa-vior, God to Thee: How Great Thou
Bb Eb Bb
Cm F7
Art, How Great Thou Art! Then sings my soul my Sa-vior, God, to
Bb Bb Eb
Bb
Thee: How Great Thou Art, How Great Thou Art!
Cm F7 Bb Eb Bb
ff
Then sings my
L

*) Play G and A with right thumb.

THE LOVE OF GOD

HAMMOND	SPINET	OTHERS
Upper: 00 8857 002	Upper: 00 8857 002	Upper: Flutes 8', 4', 2', 2 2/3'
Lower: [F♯] or [F]	Lower: 5542 0010	Lower: Strings 8', 4'
Pedal: 43	Pedal: 4	Pedal: Soft 16', 8'
Full Vibrato	Full Vibrato	Full Vibrato

F. M. LEHMAN
Arr. by Fred Bock

pure, how meas-ure - less and strong. It shall for-
Eb Cm Fm Bb7 Eb
ev - er-more en - dure the saint's and an - gels'
Ab Ab7 Eb Cm Fm Bb7
ten. A little faster
song.
Eb C G7
C Am Dm G7 C G7 C G7

mf
L
ten. ten. ten.
ten. ten. ten.
C Am Dm G7 C C7 F Fm B♭7
U
C Am Dm G7 C E7 F Fm B7
ten. Broaden
ten.
C Am Dm G7 C C B♭
ten.
a tempo
mp
Fm A♭ D♭9 E♭9 C

IN THIS VERY ROOM

Hammond Organs			Tab Organs	
Upper:	A♯ 00 6807 004		Upper:	Flutes 8′, 4′, 2′
Lower:	F♯ or 00 5624 321		Lower:	Strings and Flutes 8′, 4′
Pedal:	53		Pedal:	Flutes 16′, 8′

Words and Music by
RON and CAROL HARRIS
Arranged by Fred Bock

love for one like me, and in this ver-y room there's quite e-nough
joy for one like me; and there's quite e-nough hope, and
quite e-nough pow-er to chase a - way an - y gloom, For
Je - sus, our Lord Je - sus is in this ver-y room.
lightly rhythmic

f

Add 4′ coupler or increase
f
Gt.
mp
mp
softer
p

WHAT A FRIEND WE HAVE IN JESUS

HAMMOND ORGAN

Upper: A♯ 00 7061 400
Lower: A♯ 00 5545 111
Pedal: 51
Full Vibrato

OTHER ORGANS

Upper: Flutes 8′, $2\frac{2}{3}$
Lower: Soft Full Combination 8′, 4′
Pedal: Bourdon 16′, Flute 8′
Full Vibrato

Words and Music by
CHARLES C. CONVERSE
Arranged by Fred Bock

Tenderly, with feeling

for - feit,
Oh, what need-less pain we
bear.
All be-cause we do not
car - ry
ev - 'ry-thing to God in
prayer.
mf
ritard
Lower
slowing to the end

DAY BY DAY

HAMMOND	SPINET	OTHERS
Upper: D♯	Upper: 00 8030 000	Upper: Flute Solo 8'
Lower: E or F♯	Lower: 4432 2211	Lower: Soft Strings 8', 4'
Pedal: 54	Pedal: 5	Pedal: Light Flute & String 16'
Full Vibrato	Full Vibrato	Full Vibrato

LINA SANDELL

OSCAR AHNFELT

Arranged by Fred Bock

stow - ment, I've no cause for wor - ry or for fear. He, whose
heart is kind be-yond all meas - ure, gives to us each day what He sees
(Optional)
8va
best. Lov - ing - ly, it's part of pain and sor - row, ming-ling
(Melody)
toil with peace and rest.
ten.

GREATER IS HE THAT IS IN ME

DRAWBAR ORGANS		TAB ORGANS	
Upper:	73 7808 557	Upper:	Full organ 16', 8', 4', 2'
Lower:	00 7857 657	Lower:	Full accompaniment 8', 4'
Pedal:	53	Pedal:	Full pedal 16', 8'

Words and Music by
LANNY WOLFE
Arranged by Fred Bock

f
Upper
Lower
Upper

(like an echo)
Lower f
ff
Upper
mf

ten.
a tempo
ff
ten.
ten.
ff

JOY COMES IN THE MORNING

Hammond Organs
***Upper:** A# 00 8685 544*
***Lower:** A# 00 6645 311*
***Pedal:** 51*

Other Organs
Upper: Clarinet 8′, Flutes 4′, 2′
Lower: Strings & String Celeste 8′, Melodia 8′, Flute 4′
Pedal: Flutes 16′, 8′

Words by
WILLIAM J. and GLORIA GAITHER

Music by
WILLIAM J. GAITHER
Arranged by Fred Bock

quain - ted with sor-row, grief, or pain, But the Mas-ter prom - ised
sun-shine aft - er rain. Hold on my child, Joy comes in the
morn - ing, Weep-ing on - ly lasts for the night;
Hold on, my child, Joy comes in the morn - ing, the

lightly accented
dark-est hour means dawn is just in sight.
f
rit.
f

LOVE LIFTED ME

HAMMOND	OTHERS
Upper A# 00 7885 523	Upper Flutes 8', 4', 2⅔', 2'
Lower A# 00 5626 323	Lower Strings 8', 4', Flute 8'
Ped. 52	Ped. Flute 16', 8'
Full Vibrato	Full Vibrato

Words & Music by
James Rowe
Howard Smith
Arranged by Fred Bock

heard my des-pair-ing cry: From the wa-ters lift-ed me, now safe am I.
Love lift-ed me. Love lift-ed me. When noth-ing else could help,
Love lift-ed me. Love lift-ed me. Love lift-ed me.
When noth-ing else could help, Love lift-ed me.
f

Broaden
ff
a tempo
mf
a little faster
a tempo
f

LET'S JUST PRAISE THE LORD

Hammond Organs
Upper: ***A#*** *02 8888 002*
Lower: ***A#*** *00 6736 000*
Prepare: ***B*** *00 7848 046*
Pedal: *53*
Full Vibrato

Other Organs
Upper: Flutes 8′, 4′, $2\frac{2}{3}$′, 2′
Lower: Strings & Flutes 8′, 4′
Prepare: Full Organ, no 16′
Pedal: Flutes 16′, 8′
Full Vibrato

Words & Music By
GLORIA AND WILLIAM J. GAITHER
Arr. by Fred Bock

a little faster
f
(♩ = ♩)
no ritard!
Lower
B
Full
Organ
Upper
ff
ff

THIS IS MY COUNTRY

AL JACOBS

HAMMOND:

(A♯) 00 8888 000
Vibrato

[F] Vibrato

Ped. 43

OTHERS:

(Sw) Violin Diapason 8'
Clarinet 8', French Horn 8'
Flautino 2'

[Gt.] Flute 8', Rohr Flute 4'

Ped. Bourdon 16', Flute 8'
Gt. to Ped. 8'

R. H.
R.H.
Gt.
mf
ff

GO TELL IT ON THE MOUNTAIN

HAMMOND	SPINET	OTHERS
Upper: 00 8807 002 Full Vibrato	Upper: 00 8807 002 Full Vibrato	Upper: Flutes 8' 4' 2' Tremolo
Lower: 00 4533 220 Full Vibrato	Lower: 4533 2200 Full Vibrato	Lower: Strings 8' 4'
Pedal: 43	Pedal: 4	Pedal: Bourdon 16'

Traditional Spiritual
Arr. by Fred Bock

MOUN TAIN O-ver the hills and ev - 'ry - where
GO TELL IT ON THE MOUN TAIN that Je - sus Christ is
born.
Tenderly
r.h.
l.h.
mp
L
When I was a seek - er I
sought both night and day. I asked the Lord to

Slower
p
help me, And He showed me the way.
a tempo
ff
Go Tell It On The Moun - tain O - ver the hills and
ev - 'ry - where
Go Tell It On The Moun - tain that
Slower
Je - sus Christ is born.

HEALER OF BROKEN HEARTS

DRAWBAR ORGANS		TAB ORGANS	
Upper:	00 7563 523	Upper:	Flutes 8', 4', Clarinet 8', Oboe 8'
Lower:	00 4624 000	Lower:	Soft String ensemble 8', 4'
Pedal:	41	Pedal:	Light Flutes 16', 8'

Words and Music by
GEORGIA STIFFLER
Arranged by Fred Bock

Upper
mf
you ev - 'ry sor - row has borne. He's the heal - er of
bro - ken hearts, He'll mend your shat - tered
dreams. He'll pick up the threads of your bro - ken
smoothly
life, and weave them to - geth - er a - gain.

To your soul He'll bring peace and joy,
f
A friend in need He'll be; The
heal - er of bro - ken hearts is Je - sus of
ritard
white key glissando
Gal - li - lee.
f
mf
white pedal glissando

I'LL TELL THE WORLD

HAMMOND
Upper A# 00 7471 720
Lower A# 00 6745 222
Prepare Lower B 00 6816 434
Ped. 52
Full Vibrato

OTHERS
Upper Clarinet 8'
Flute 4'
Lower Straight Flutes 8'
Ped. Bourdon 16'
Full Vibrato

Words and Music by
Baynard L. Fox
Arranged by Fred Bock

Add 4' Flute
Hammond Lower B
a bit faster
Christ - ian; I'll take Him with me an - y - where.
f
I'll tell the
f
world how Je - sus saved me, and how He gave me a life brand new;
And I know that if you trust Him that all He gave me, He'll give to you.
Upper
I'll tell the world that He's my Sav - ior, No oth - er

one could love me so. My life, my all, is His for -
ev - er, And where He leads me, I will go.
Lower
f

Upper
f
Lower
mp
Upper
ten.
ten.
ten.

HE TOUCHED ME

HAMMOND	SPINET	OTHERS
Upper: 00 8877 002 Full Vibrato	Upper: 00 8877 002 Full Vibrato	Upper: Strings, Flutes 8', 4' Full Vibrato
Lower: F♯ Full Vibrato	Lower: 4454 3010 Full Vibrato	Lower: Flutes 8', Strings 4' Full Vibrato
Pedal: 54	Pedal: 5	Pedal: Bourdon 16', Flute 8'

Words and Music by
WILLIAM J. GAITHER
Arr. by Fred Bock

U
shame.
mf
Then the hand of
Je - sus touched me and now I am no
long - er the same.
A little faster

mf
f
He
Touched Me,
O, He
Touched Me
and

O, the joy that floods my soul.
Some - thing hap - pened and now I know, He
ten.
Touched Me, and made me whole.
ff

Broaden slightly
ff
L
mf

I CANNOT FAIL THE LORD

HAMMOND	SPINET	OTHERS
Upper: 77 5505 005 Full Vibrato	Upper: 77 5505 005 Full Vibrato	Upper: Flutes 16', 8', 4', 2 2/3' Also Mixture 5 1/3' Full Vibrato
Lower: F or G Full Vibrato	Lower: 5606 4300 Full Vibrato	Lower: Flutes & Strings 8' Full Vibrato
Pedal: 52	Pedal: 5	Pedal: Flutes 16', 8'

DORIS AKERS
Arr. by Fred Bock

Warmly

LORD. And things when done in His name are
won in the past I did - n't trust God. I
trust - ed in my - self, Now I know I have His help, And I CAN - NOT
FAIL THE LORD.
L f I
Strongly
CAN - NOT FAIL THE

LORD. I CAN - NOT FAIL THE LORD.
U mp
He has nev er failed me yet Ev - 'ry prob - lem He has met
Slower
f
And I
1
CAN - NOT FAIL THE LORD.
L
2
ten.
CAN - NOT FAIL THE LORD.
pp

HE'S EVERYTHING TO ME

HAMMOND ORGAN
Upper: A♯ 02 8480 500
Prepare: B 55 7706 225
Lower: A♯ 00 5645 332
Pedal: 50
Vibrato 1

OTHER ORGANS
Upper: Clarinet 8′
Prepare: Full Flute Chorus 16′ 8′, 4′, 2′
Lower: Strings, Diapasons 8′, 4′,
Pedal: Light 16′
Small Vibrato

Words and Music by
RALPH CARMICHAEL
Arranged by Fred Bock

Tho' He rul-eth o - ver land and sea,
f What is that to me?
Lower
Upper
mf I will cel - e - brate na - ti - vi - ty,
For it has a place in his - to - ry,
Sure, He came to set His peo - ple free,
What is that to

Add: Full Vibrato
me?
'Til by faith I met Him face to face,
And I felt the won-der of His grace,
Then I knew that He was
more than just a God who did-n't care, Who lived a-way up there, And,
now He walks be-side me day by day,
Ev-er watch-ing o'er me

lest I stray,
Help - ing me to find that nar - row way,
He's ev - 'ry thing to me.

Change to other registration
8va
Broaden
8va
ten.
Upper
ff
ten.
fff
Increase Pedal 5
ff

TO BE USED OF GOD

HAMMOND

Upper: 03 6678 322
Full Vibrato
Lower: 00 5644 330
Full Vibrato
Pedal: 50

SPINET

Upper: 03 6678 322
Full Vibrato
Lower: 5644 3300
Full Vibrato
Pedal: 5

OTHERS

Upper: Flutes 8', 4', 2', 2 2/3'
Full Vibrato
Lower: Strings 8', 4'
Full Vibrato
Pedal: Bourdon 16', Flute 8'

AUDREY MIEIR
Arr. by Fred Bock

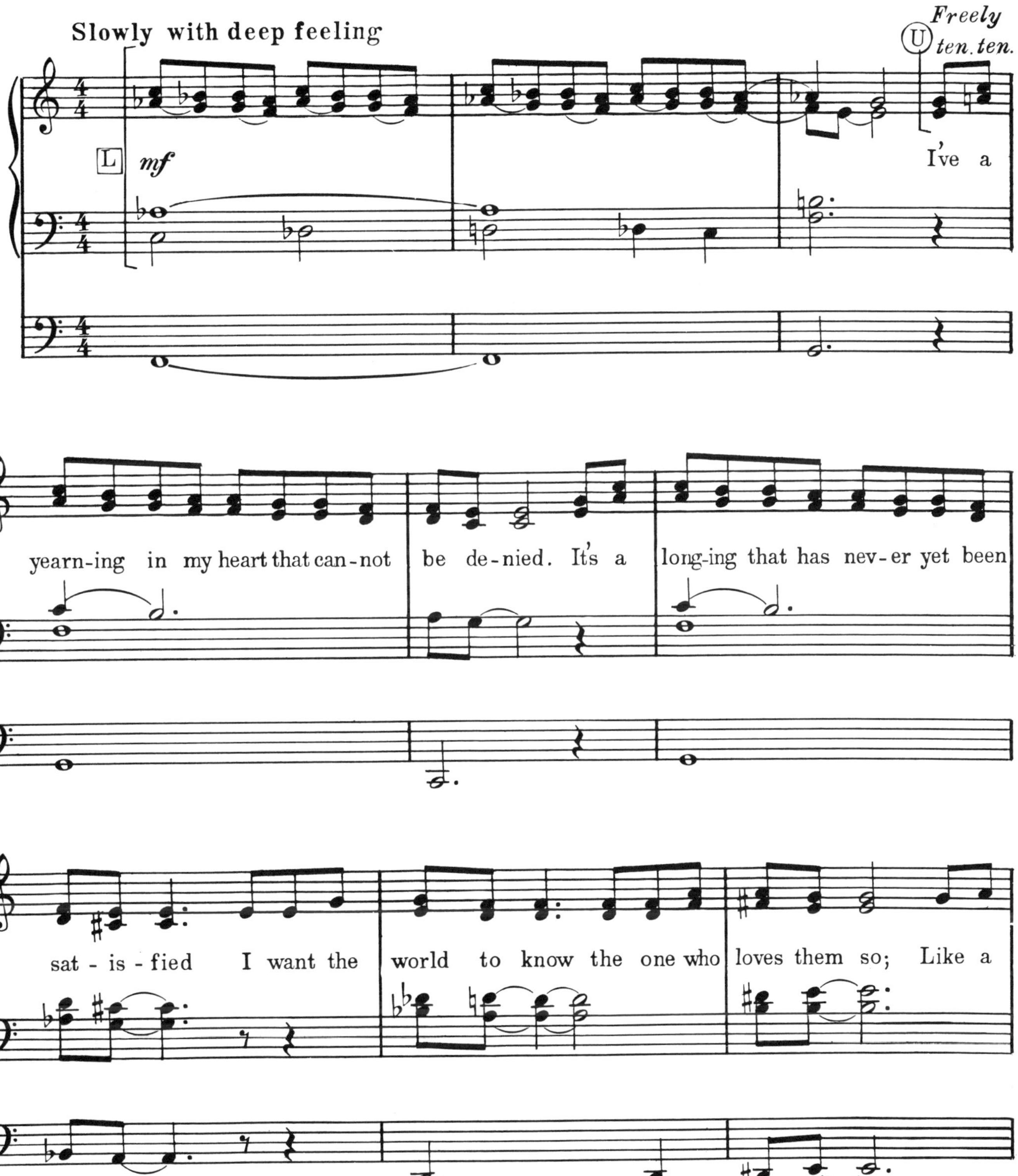

flame it's burn-ing deep in - side. When I think a-bout the short-ness of my
earth-ly years, I re - mem-ber all the wast-ed days, the wast - ed tears, I long to
preach the Word to those who've nev - er heard of the One who can dis-pel all
In a light tempo
ten. ten.
fears. To Be Used Of God To sing, to speak, to
ten. ten.

pray
To Be Used Of God to show some-one the
way
I long so much to feel the touch of
His con - sum - ing fire; To Be Used Of God is my de -
sire.
ff
mf
ten. ten. ten.
ten.
ten.

WHEN HE SHALL COME

HAMMOND	OTHERS
Upper D# or 00 8302 000	Upper Flute, 8'
Lower G or 00 6727 323	Lower Strings and Flutes 8', 4'
Ped. 54	Ped. Bourdon 16'
Full Vibrato	Full Vibrato

Words & Music by
Almeda J. Pearce
Arranged by Fred Bock

Warmly *ad lib.*

walk with Him in white.
Lower
Upper
a little faster
ten.
ten.
Lower

NEARER, MY GOD, TO THEE

DRAWBAR ORGANS		TAB ORGANS	
Upper:	01 7050 200	Upper:	Strings, String Celeste 8', 4'
Lower:	00 3504 001	Lower:	Flutes 8', 4'
Pedal:	31	Pedal:	Flute 16'

Words and Music by
SARAH F. ADAMS and LOWELL MASON
Arranged by Fred Bock

p
Upper
Lower

SWEET, SWEET SPIRIT

HAMMOND ORGANS

Upper: A♯ 01 8848 221
Lower: A♯ 00 5634 221
Pedal: 51
Full Vibrato

OTHER ORGANS

Upper: Flutes 8', 4', 2 '
Lower: Strings & Flutes 8', 4'
Pedal: Light Flutes 16', 8'
Full Vibrato

Arr. by Fred Bock

Words and Music by
DORIS AKERS

And I
know that it's the
Spir - it of the Lord.
Upper
3
Lower
There are
sweet ex -
- pres - sions on each
face,
and I
know they feel the
pres - ence of the Lord.

Upper
Sweet Ho - ly Spir - it, Sweet Heav-en - ly
Dove, Stay right here with us,
Fill-ing us with your love. And for these

bright and rhythmic
bless - ings we lift our heart's in praise. With - out a
doubt we'll know that we have been re - vived when
we shall leave this place.
1
2
7
thumb gliss.
ten.
ten.
thumb gliss.
8va
ten.
ten.

PLENTY OF ROOM IN THE FAMILY

Other Organs
Upper: Flutes 8′, 4′, 2⅔′, 2′
Strings 8′, 4′
Lower: Strings & Flutes 8′, 4′
Flute Celeste 8′
Pedal: Flutes 16′, 8′

Hammond Organs
Upper: A♯ 00 8885 453
Lower: A♯ 00 5645 321
Pedal: 62

Words by
WILLIAM J. and GLORIA GAITHER

Music by
WILLIAM J. GAITHER
Arranged by Fred Bock

Bright 'n' happy

plen-ty be-sides and the store-house will nev - er be bare.
smoother
mf
Full vibrato on
Plen-ty of room in the fam - 'ly, room for the young and the old.

Plen-ty of hap - pi-ness,
plen-ty of love,
Plen-ty of room in the fold.
Upper:
rit.
f

OH, I NEVER SHALL FORGET THE DAY

HAMMOND	SPINET	OTHERS
Upper: 00 8808 023 Vib. 3	Upper: 00 8808 023 Vib. 3	Upper: Tibia 8' 4' 2' Vibrato
Lower: 00 6624 211 Vib. 3	Lower: 6624 2110 Vib. 3	Lower: Flutes 8' 4' Vibrato
Pedal: 52	Pedal: 4	Pedal: Tibia 16' Bourdon 16' Gt. to Ped.

Arranged by
FRED BOCK

RALPH CARMICHAEL

Fm Bb Eb7 With feeling
last I found a friend - ship true. First He
mf
Ab Db Eb Fm Eb ten.
brushed a - way the clouds of fear, and gave to me a song, Then He
Ao D7 Gm Fm Bb ten.
prom - ised al - ways to be near, and keep me from all wrong. Oh, I
Eb D7 Db7 C7
nev - er shall for - get the day that Je - sus took my sin a - way, and

Fm Bb7 Eb G+
He will do the same for you. I can
mp
Ab Db Eb Fm Eb ten. A° D7
trust in His un-chang-ing love for it will nev-er die, 'Til the day He calls me home a-bove to
Gm Gb+ Fm E7 Eb D7
dwell with Him on high. Oh, I nev - er shall for - get the hour, His
ff
Broaden
Db7 C7 Fm Bb Eb
sav - ing grace, His cleans-ing pow'r re - deemed my soul and set me free!
ff

SWEETER AS THE YEARS GO BY

HAMMOND
(U)pper: (A#) 00 7005 002
[L]ower: [A#] 00 4422 111
Pedal: 42
Full vibrato

OTHERS
(U)pper: Flutes 8', 2'
[L]ower: Strings 8', 4'
Pedal: Light Flute 16'
Full vibrato

Words and Music by
Mrs. C. H. MORRIS
Arr. by Fred Bock

sea, And high - er than the heav - ens My theme shall ev - er
D7 Gm B♭7 E♭ F7 B♭ E♭ B♭ F7
be.
not too fast
Sweet - er as the years go by,
B♭ F7 B♭ C7
Sweet-er as the years go by;
F7 A7 B♭
Rich - er, full - er, deep - er,
B♭7
Je - sus' love is sweet - er,
E♭
Sweet-er as the years go by.
B♭ Gm C7 F7 B♭ E♭7 (sus) E♭7

A♭ B♭7 E♭7 G7(-5) A♭
faster
A♭maj7 A♭7
D♭ F7 B♭m G♭7 A♭ E♭7(sus) C7
ff
L
mf
Fm D♭m7 A♭ E♭7(sus) E♭7 A♭

YESTERDAY, TODAY AND TOMORROW

HAMMOND ORGAN
Upper: B 78 8270 000
Prepare: A♯ 78 8767 346
Lower: B 00 5805 000
Prepare: A♯ 00 7857 335
Pedal: 51
Vibrato 1

OTHER ORGANS
Upper: Flutes 16′, 5⅓, 8′, 2⅔
Prepare: Full Organ, with 16′
Lower: Flutes & Strings 8′ 4′
Prepare: Full Organ, no 16′
Pedal: Gt. to Ped. 8′
Bourdon 16′, Flute 16′, 8′
Small Vibrato

Words and Music by
DON WYRTZEN
Arranged by Fred Bock

*) Play with right thumb

To - day,
To - day,
To - day He
lives for me,
To - day,
To-day He
lives for me,
lives __ for me,
This is
vic - to -
Brightly
Full Organ
ry.
Lower
f
To-mor-row He
comes for me,
He comes,
He comes,
To-mor-row He
comes for me,
He comes,
To-mor-row He

comes for me, Comes for me, This is mys-ter - y.
Full Organ setting
Upper
ff
O, friend, do you know Him? Know Him, Know Him,
O, friend, do you know Him? Know Him, O, friend, do you know Him, do
Broaden
you know Him? Je-sus Christ, Je-sus Christ, Je-sus Christ, the Lord.
ff

MY HEART IS FILLED WITH JESUS' LOVE

HAMMOND ORGANS

Upper: A♯ 00 7777 001

Lower: A♯ 00 4543 112
Pedal: 52
Full Vibrato

OTHER ORGANS

Upper: Full Flute Chorus 8', 4', 2⅔', 2'
Lower: Strings 8', 4'
Pedal: Light Flutes 16', 8'
Full Vibrato

Arr. by Fred Bock

Words and Music by
DORIS AKERS

dove, de - scends on me, de - scends on me. The
sweet - ness of His pow'r di - vine
is bless - ing me, is bless - ing me. To
know I'm His and He is mine

1
Upper
sweeps o - ver
me,
sweeps o - ver
me.
Lower
2
Upper
Lower
Upper
ten.
ten.

I'LL FLY AWAY

HAMMOND
Upper A# 00 7507 331
Lower A# 00 8030 000
(Prepare) B 01 6847 335
Ped. 53
Small Vibrato (to start)

OTHERS
Upper Flutes 8', 4', 2'
Lower Flute 8' or Tibia 8'
(Prepare) Full Ensemble but upper keyboard should still be dominant.
Ped. Flutes 16', 8'
Small Vibrato (to start)

Words & Music by
Albert Brumley
Arranged by Fred Bock

Ad lib, meditatively

When I die, hal-le- lu-jah, by and by, I'll fly a - way.
Bright and happy
twice as fast
1st time-No Vibrato
2nd time-Full Vibrato
Play cue notes on second repeat
Upper
f
Lower
Smoothly
Upper
Lower
1

2
Broaden 2nd repeat only
(2nd repeat only)
Hammond: B
Others: Full ensemble
Lower
ff
(2nd repeat only)
legato
Upper
f
Upper
Lower
f
1 2 3 1 2 3 4

HEAVEN CAME DOWN AND GLORY FILLED MY SOUL

HAMMOND	SPINET	OTHERS
(U)–02 8888 002	(U)–02 8888 002	(U)–Flute 8'-4'-2'-2⅔'
[L] - [F]	[L]–6443 3220	[L]–Strings & Flutes 8'-4'
Ped.–54	Ped.–4 or 5	Ped.–Flutes 16'-8'
Full Vibrato	Full Vibrato	Full Vibrato

JOHN W. PETERSON
Arr. by Fred Bock

Brightly *(one to a bar)*

U
U
L

rit.
much slower

(♮)
L
U

U
U
L
ten. ten.
smoothly
gliss.
ff
ten.
ten.
ten.
U

THE CHURCH TRIUMPHANT

Hammond Organs
Upper: B 46 8646 421
Percussion: on, normal, fast, second
Prepare: A♯ 73 7848 436
Lower: 00 6716 110
(use F pre-set on intro. & ending)
Pedal: 50

Other Organs
Upper: Clarinet 8′, Flutes 16′, 4′
Percussion on, fast decay
Prepare: Full Ensemble: 16′, 8′, 4′, 2′
Lower: Soft Flutes 8′, 4′, Flute Celeste 8′
Pedal: Bourdon 16′, Light Flute 8′

Words and Music by
WILLIAM J. and GLORIA GAITHER
Arranged by Fred Bock

choice; Let the an - them ring out, songs of vic - to - ry
to Coda
swell, For the church tri - um-phant is a - live and
Upper: Full ensemble, A♯
f
l. h.
well. This ol' ship's been thru some bat-tles be-
fore, Storms and tem-pest and rocks on the shore. Tho' the

hull may be bat-tered, in - side it's safe and dry, It will
car-ry its car-go to the port in the sky.
Upper: Percussion, B
Lower
CODA
Upper: Full Ensemble, A♯
slower
Vibrato off
Lower
mf
ten. ten.
very slowly
ten. ten.
ten.

I'VE GOT PEACE LIKE A RIVER

HAMMOND	SPINET	OTHERS
Upper: (A#) 00 8808 003 Vibrato 3	Upper: 00 8808 003 Full Vibrato	Upper: Flutes 8', 4', 2' Full Vibrato
Lower: [F]	Lower: 5524 3001	Lower: Strings & Flutes 8'
Pedal: 42	Pedal: 4	Pedal: Bourdon 16', Flute 8'

SPIRITUAL
Arr. by Fred Bock

RIV - ER I GOT PEACE LIKE A RIV - ER in - a my soul.
L Smoothly (Soft Flute or G♯)
p
mf
U
I've got joy like a riv - er, I've got joy like a riv - er, I've got joy like a riv - er in my soul.
I've got

joy like a riv- er, I've got joy like a
riv- er, I've got joy like a riv - er in my
soul.
U
I've got
L
love like a
riv- er, I've got love like a riv- er, I've got

love like a riv er in my soul.
I've got love like a riv - er, I got
joy like a riv - er, I've got peace like a
riv - er in my soul, in my soul!
rit.

THE UNVEILED CHRIST

HAMMOND		OTHERS	
Ⓤpper:	Ⓐ♯ 00 8846 006 Vibrato 1	Ⓤpper:	Flutes 8', 4', 2⅔' Small vibrato
[L]ower:	[A♯] 00 5665 000 Vibrato off	[L]ower:	String 8', 4' No vibrato
Pedal:	43	Pedal:	Bourdon 16'

Words and Music by
N. B. HERRELL
Arr. by Fred Bock

two.
Cm
E♭
B♭7
E♭
Cm
B♭7/E♭
E♭
Full vibrato on
f
Oh, be - hold the Man of Sor - rows!
A♭
E♭

Oh, be-hold Him in plain view!
Lo! He is the mighty
Cm Fsus F7 B♭7 B♭+ E♭7(sus) A+
Con - qu'ror, Since He rent the veil in two.
A♭ F7 E♭ B♭7 E♭ E♭7
Lo! He is the might-y Con - qu'ror, Since He rent the veil in
A♭ E♭ B♭sus B♭7
two.
f
E♭ A♭ E♭

Cm
F7
B♭
B♭+
E♭(sus)
E♭9
f
A♭
F7(sus)
F7
E♭
B♭7
E♭
E♭7
A♭
ff
E♭
mf
Fm
B♭7(sus)
B♭7
p
pp
E♭

LOVE AT HOME

HAMMOND

Upper: 00 8808 023
Vib. 3
Lower: 00 6624 211
Vib. 3
Pedal: 52

SPINET

Upper: 00 8808 023
Vib. 3
Lower: 6624 2110
Vib. 3
Pedal: 4

OTHERS

Upper: Tibia 8' 4' 2'
Vibrato
Lower: Flutes 8' 4'
Vibrato
Pedal: Tibia 16' Bourdon 16'
Gt. to Ped.

Adapted and Arranged by
WILLIAM KING DRIGGS Jr.
Organ Arr. by Fred Bock

Smil - ing sweet on ev 'ry side. Time doth soft - ly, sweet - ly glide
When there's LOVE AT HOME LOVE AT HOME
f ten. ten.
LOVE AT HOME
ten.
Time doth soft - ly, sweet - ly glide
ten.
Slower
ten.
p
When there's LOVE AT HOME,
ten.
When there's LOVE AT HOME.
ten.

THANK GOD FOR THE PROMISE OF SPRING

Hammond Organs
Upper: *A# 00 8080 604*
Lower: *A# 00 6745 221*
Pedal: *42*

Other Organs
Upper: Clarinet 8′, Flutes 4′, 2′
Stopped Diapason 8′
Lower: Strings, Melodia 8′, 4′
Pedal: Bourdon 16′, Flute 8′

Words by
WILLIAM J. and GLORIA GAITHER

Music by
WILLIAM J. GAITHER
Arranged by Fred Bock

Moderato

shad - ows, And His smile can't be far a - way.
lightly rhythmic
Thank God for the prom-ise of Spring-time, Once a -
gain my heart will sing; There's a brand new
day a - dawn - ing, Thank God for the prom - ise of

ten. ten.
a tempo
Spring.
ten. ten.
f
ten.
ten.
p
mp
reduce pedal

SAVIOR, LIKE A SHEPHERD LEAD US

HAMMOND ORGANS

Upper: 00 8006 000
Lower: F ♯ or 00 5430 001
Pedal: 41
Full Vibrato

ALL ORGANS

Upper: Flutes 8′, 2′
Lower: Strings 8′, 4′
Pedal: Soft Flute 16′
Full Vibrato

WILLIAM BRADBURY
Arr. by Fred Bock

mf

a little faster
rit.
mp a tempo
R. H. play
up stems
pp

THE MIRACLE OF GRACE

DRAWBAR ORGANS		TAB ORGANS	
Upper:	(G♯) or (F♯) preset light vibrato	Upper:	Oboe 8', light vibrato
Prepare: (A♯)	02 6807 006	Prepare:	Full Flute Chorus 8', 4', 2'
Lower: (F♯)	preset	Lower:	Strings & Flutes 8', 4'
Pedal:	43	Pedal:	Flutes 16', 8', Couple Lower to Pedal 8'

Words and Music by
RALPH CARMICHAEL
Arranged by Fred Bock

might - y o - ceans roar, And far a - way new
pla - ces to ex - plore. But
Full vibrato on Full Flutes
A♯
all these won - ders, great or small, are mere re - flec - tions
of the great - est won - der of them all, the

*Play on lower manual with right hand.

GOD LEADS HIS DEAR CHILDREN ALONG

HAMMOND ORGAN
Upper: A♯ 00 6225 000
Lower: A♯ 00 5604 002
Pedal: 51
Full Vibrato

OTHER ORGANS
Upper: Flutes 8′, 2′
Lower: Strings, 8′, 4′, 2′
Pedal: Bourdon 16′
Full Vibrato

Words and Music by
G. A. YOUNG
Arranged by Fred Bock

feet God leads His dear child-ren a - long
Some thro' the wa - ters, Some thro' the flood, Some thro' the
Upper
fire, But all thro' the blood Some thro' great sor - row, But
Lower
ten.
ten.
God gives a song, In the night sea-son and all the day
ten.
ten.

*) Left Hand play entire chord.

HAPPINESS

HAMMOND
Upper: (A♯) 57 6608 002
prepare: (B) 00 7800 060
Percussion: On, normal, fast, second
Lower: 00 6725 002
Pedal: 52
Light Vibrato

OTHERS
Upper: Flutes 5⅓', 16', 8', 2'
Percussion: On, fast decay
Lower: Strings & Flutes 8', 4'
Pedal: Flutes 16', 8'
Small Vibrato

Words and Music by
WILLIAM J. GAITHER
Arr. by Fred Bock

cord. I found hap - pi - ness all the time, won - der - ful peace of mind,
When I found the Lord.
smoothly
smoothly
Slowing, greatly
No more lone - ly days of pain and mis - er - y,
Lower
For the door of hap - pi - ness I've found the key.

I have found a life of love and har - mo - ny,
Slowly and warmly
Won - drous hap - pi - ness all the time,
ten.
har - mo - ny so di - vine,
ten.
since I found the Lord!
Upper
Percussion on
a tempo
3

1
smoothly
2
Broaden

OVER THE SUNSET MOUNTAINS

HAMMOND	SPINET	OTHERS
(U) – 00 7707 002	(U) – 00 7707 002	(U) – Flutes 8′-4′-2′
[L] – [F♯]	[L] – 5544 3300	[L] – Strings 8′-4′
Ped.– 53	Ped.– 4	Ped.– Soft 16′
Full Vibrato	Full Vibrato	Full Vibrato

JOHN W. PETERSON
Arr. by Fred Bock

smoothly
f

rit.
mp
8va
L
U
8va
(loco)
a tempo
p
mf
f
mp
p
pp
ppp

PRECIOUS MEMORIES

Suggested Registration
For General Electronic or Pipe Organs
Upper: Flutes 16', 4'
Lower: String Diapason 8'
Pedal: 16', 8', Medium

Suggested Registration
For Pre-Set Organs
(A#) 60 0722 000
(B) 08 8500 000
[A#] 00 5533 000

Suggested Registration
For Spinet Drawbar Organs
(U) 60 0722 000
[L] 5533 0000
Pedal 3
Vibrato On, Normal

J. B. WRIGHT
Arranged by Fred Bock

And the sac - red past un - fold.
In gentle rhythm
Prec - ious mem - 'ries, how they lin - ger how they ev - er flood my soul.
U
L
p
in mf the
L

still - ness of the mid - night,
Pre - cious, sa - cred scenes un - fold.
f ff
in the still-ness of the
Slower
mid - night, prec - ious, sa-cred scenes un - fold.
tr

HE IS WITH ME

HAMMOND	SPINET	OTHERS
(U) – 00 8867 323	(U) – 00 8867 323	(U) – Flutes & Strings 8'-4'-2'
[L] – [F♯]	[L] – 5544 2220	[L] – Accompaniment 8'
Ped.– 53	Ped.– 4	Ped.– Bourdon 16'-8'
Full Vibrato	Full Vibrato	Full Vibrato

JOHN W. PETERSON
Arr. by Fred Bock

Tenderly, with feeling

ten.ten.
ten.
ten.
ten.
a little brighter
f
broaden
pp

I BELIEVE IN A HILL CALLED MT. CALVARY

Hammond Organs
Upper: A# 01 8808 005
Lower: A# 00 6745 224
Pedal: 53
Full Vibrato

Other Organs
Upper: Flutes 8′, 4′, 2′
Lower: Strings 8′, 4′, Light Flute or Stopped Diapason 8′
Pedal: Bourdon 16′, Flute 8′
Full Vibrato

Words By
DALE OLDHAM,
GLORIA AND WILLIAM J. GAITHER

Music By
WILLIAM J. GAITHER
Arr. by Fred Bock

old rug - ged cross.
Lower
I be - lieve that the

Christ who was slain on the cross, Has the pow - er to
change lives to - day. For He changed me com -
plete - ly, And a new life is mine; That is why by the
cross I will stay.
Upper

Lower
mp
Upper
mp

THE BLOOD WILL NEVER LOSE ITS POWER

HAMMOND ORGANS

Upper: A♯ 00 8770 333
Lower: A♯ 00 5434 221
Pedal: 52
Full Vibrato

OTHER ORGANS

Upper: Flutes 8', 4', 2⅔'
Lower: Strings & Flutes 8', 4'
Pedal: Light Flutes 16', 8'
Full Vibrato

Arr. by Fred Bock

Words and Music by
ANDRAÉ CROUCH

day to day, It will nev - er
lose it's pow'r. It
reach - es to the high - est moun - tain,
It flows to the low - est val - ley;

The blood that gives me strength from
day to day It will nev - er
lose its pow'r.
a little faster
f

slowing
ff
Upper

EVEN SO, LORD JESUS, COME

HAMMOND
Upper: 00 8885 113
Lower: 00 7705 110
Pedal: 52
Full Vibrato

OTHERS
Upper: Flutes 8', 4', 2⅔', 2'
Lower: Flutes & Strings 8', 4'
Pedal: 16', 8'
Full Vibrato

Words by WILLIAM J. GAITHER and GLORIA GAITHER

Music by WILLIAM J. GAITHER
Arr. by Fred Bock

need Thy rich in - fill - ing, E - ven
Upper
light rhythm
so, Lord Je - sus, come. E - ven
so, Lord Je - sus, come, My
heart doth long for Thee! though I've

failed and be - trayed Thy trust, E - ven so, Lord
Je - sus, come!
Brighter
f

a bit faster
Lower
ten.
ten.
ten.

JESUS IS COMING AGAIN

HAMMOND
Upper: 00 8877 002
Full Vibrato
Lower: F♯
Full Vibrato
Pedal: 54

SPINET
Upper: 00 8877 002
Full Vibrato
Lower: 4454 3010
Full Vibrato
Pedal: 5

OTHERS
Upper: Strings, Flutes 8', 4'
Full Vibrato
Lower: Flutes 8', Strings 4'
Full Vibrato
Pedal: Bourdon 16', Flute 8'

Words and Music by
JOHN W. PETERSON
Arr. by Fred Bock

com - ing a - gain
U
Dm7 G C C C7 F F♯o
Oh what a won-der-ful day it will be!
JE-SUS IS COM-ING A - GAIN.
L
rit.
rubato
L Mar-vel-ous mes-sage we
mp
C Dm7 G7 C Am D7 G7 C
bring, Glo-ri-ous car-ol we sing, Won-der-ful word of the
F A7 D7 G G9 E7
U a tempo
King, JE-SUS IS COM-ING A - GAIN. Com - ing a-
mf
Am A♭7 C G7 C A♭7 D♭

gain, com - ing a - gain, May - be morn - ing,
L
U
Ebm7 Ab7 Ebm7 Ab Db Eo
may - be noon, may - be eve-ning and may - be soon!
Com - ing a-
U
L
Ebm7 Ab+ Db Ab7 Db
Add 16' to U (or first brown tone bar)
gain, com - ing a - gain, Oh, what a won-der-ful
U
f
Ebm7 Ab7 Ebm7 Ab Db Db Db7
day it will be! JE - SUS IS COM - ING A - GAIN!
ff
Gb Go Db Ebm7 Ab7 Db A Ab Db

HE'LL NEVER LET YOU FALL

HAMMOND	SPINET	OTHERS
Upper: 02 6888 662 No Vibrato	Upper: 02 6888 662 No Vibrato	Upper: Sax. 8' Eng. Hrn. 8' Oboe 8' No Vibrato
Lower: 00 6624 000 No Vibrato	Lower: 6624 0000 No Vibrato	Lower: Flutes 8' 4' No Vibrato
Pedal: 53	Pedal: 5	Pedal: Gt. to Ped. Tibia 16'
Prepare: Upp. 80 8808 005	Prepare: Upp. Full Ensemble Pre-set	Prepare: Upp. Full Flutes Full Vibrato

Arranged by
FRED BOCK

RALPH CARMICHAEL

F
But to ev - 'ry one of us, wheth - er great or small,
B♭ B° F Dm G7 C7
He gives the cour - age to be brave, Hell nev - er let you
Change to Full Flute Ensemble
80 8808 005
U B♭7 F
fall. Da - vid up and slew his gi - ants, 'Ze - kiel's bones just
f
F7 B♭7
walked a - way! Lock - jaw stopped those hun - gry li - ons,

As in the begining
Vibrato off
U
G7 C F
Ste - phen's gon - na wear a crown some day. So to ev - 'ry
one of us, wheth-er great or small,
B♭ B°
He gives the cour - age
F Dm G7 C7 F D7 G7 C7
to be brave,___ He'll nev - er let you fall. He watch - es o - ver
F D7 Gm D7 Gm D7 Gm G♭7 F
all. He will nev-er let you fall.
ten.
ppp
f

AMEN!

HAMMOND

Upper: 00 7817 224
Vib. 3
Lower: 00 5523 200
Vib. 3
Pedal: 42

SPINET

Upper: 00 7817 224
Vib. 3
Lower: 5523 2000
Vib. 3
Pedal: 4

OTHERS

Upper: Tibia 8' 4' 2'
Salicional 8' Vibrato
Lower: Flutes 8'
Vibrato
Pedal: Tibia 16'

Traditional Spiritual
Arr. by Fred Bock

Now there's wis - dom
A - - MEN A - -
MEN, A - MEN, A - MEN.
A - - MEN! A - -
MEN! A - - MEN, A -
3

MEN, A - MEN!
A - -
MEN.
A - -
MEN
A - -
MEN A - MEN
A - -
MEN.
L